THE PROTOCOL SCHOOL OF WASHINGTON®

THE POWER OF HANDSHAKING

Also by Dorothea Johnson

Entertaining and Etiquette for Today (ACROPOLIS, 1979)

The Little Book of Etiquette (RUNNING PRESS, 1997)

Tea & Etiquette (CAPITAL BOOKS, INC., 1998)

THE PROTOCOL SCHOOL OF WASHINGTON®

THE POWER OF HANDSHAKING

FOR PEAK PERFORMANCE WORLDWIDE

ROBERT E. BROWN AND DOROTHEA JOHNSON

ILLUSTRATIONS BY CHARLIE POWELL

A CAPITAL IDEAS BOOK

Capital Books, Inc.
Sterling, Virginia

Capital Books, Inc.
P.O. Box 605
Herndon, Virginia 20172-0605

ISBN 1-931868-88-3 (alk.paper)

This publication is designed to provide accurate and authoritative information with regard to the subject matter covered. It is sold with the understanding that the publisher is not engaged in rendering legal, accounting, or other professional advice. If legal advice or other expert assistance is required, the services of a competent professional person should be sought.
— From a *Declaration of Principles* jointly adopted by a Committee of the American Bar Association and a Committee of Publishers and Associations.

Capital Books, Inc., books are available at special quantity discounts to use in corporate training programs, or for use as premiums and sales promotions. For more information, please write to Kathleen Hughes at Capital Books.

Illustrations © Charlie Powell, an illustrator in Santa Cruz, California. His work has appeared in many magazines nationwide. He can be reached at his website: www.charliepowell.net

Designed by: Rose Storey—who can be reached at her website: www.RoseStorey.com

Library of Congress Cataloging-in-Publication Data

Brown, Robert E. (Robert Edward), 1936-
 The power of handshaking : for peak performance worldwide / Robert E.
Brown and Dorothea Johnson ; Illustrations by Charlie Powell—1st ed.
 p. cm.
 Includes bibliographical references and index.
 ISBN 1-931868-88-3
 1. Business etiquette. 2. Handshaking. 3. Interpersonal communication. I. Johnson, Dorothea,
1929—II. Title.

HF5389.B769 2004
395.5'2--dc22

2004009880

Printed in the United States of America on acid-free paper that meets the American National Standards Institute Z39-48 Standard.

First Edition

10 9 8 7 6 5 4 3 2 1

To my wife, Doris. Thank you.

ROBERT E. BROWN

To my granddaughter Liv Tyler,
a world-class handshaker

DOROTHEA JOHNSON

CONTENTS

ACKNOWLEDGMENTS

Sincere thanks to our editorial and production team of Ann Noyes, Jeane Anderson, Heather Noyes, Noemi C. Arthur, and especially to Dan Imhoff for his contributions to the story line.

Also, much appreciation to Kathleen Hughes, our patient publisher, who believed in us, and Rose-Marie Robinson (Kiwi) for bringing two handshaking veterans together. And finally, to all our clients and colleagues who know the power of handshaking.

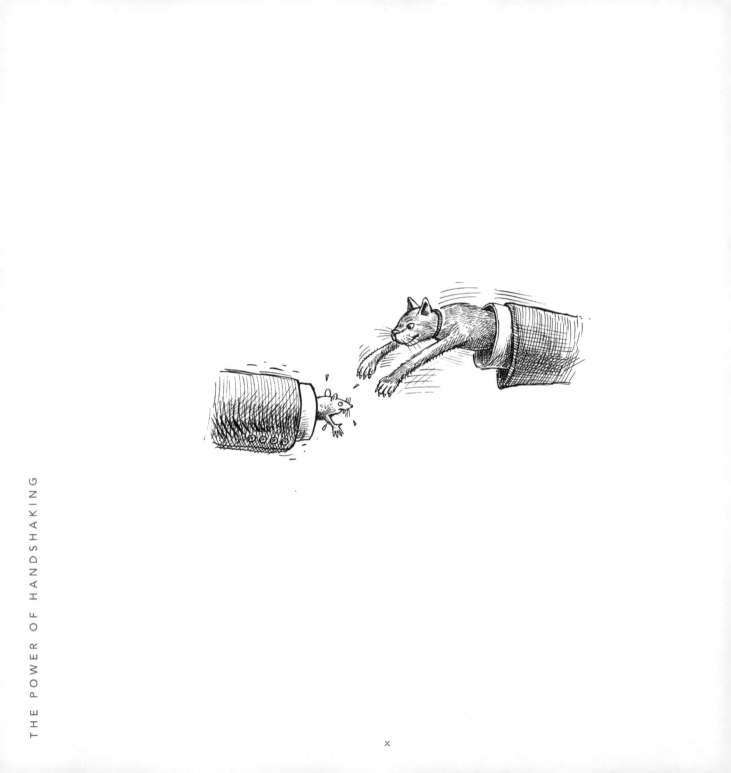

x

INTRODUCTION

WELCOME TO THE POWER OF HANDSHAKING

A doctor once wrote to Miss Manners in her syndicated column that the ritual of handshaking was a barbaric male-generated custom that merely helped the spread of disease. She refused to shake hands with people whom she met—occasionally she was prodded into the act but resented it deeply—and couldn't understand why this outdated custom did not disappear.

Yes, handshaking is a ritual. Yes, it was begun and originally practiced by men hundreds of years ago. But it is not outdated. And it is not barbaric—in fact, its roots are in building bridges between people, thereby reducing barbarism.

But more importantly, handshaking is a valuable form of nonverbal communication. It is a form of interactive body language that offers insights into how the other person views the world, him or herself, and you. It is a vital, if usually subconscious, part of creating a first impression and sending a parting message.

Learning to consciously send the message you want to convey and interpret the subconscious messages you receive is valuable to both your business and personal lives. Doctors can learn a great deal about patients and patients can understand more about their physicians. Salespeople, investment bankers, their clients, teachers, managers, politicians, new friends and co-workers—all engage in this custom and all can benefit from understanding the meanings and messages of handshakes.

What about the argument that it spreads germs? Yes, it is possible to pass colds and other germs hand-to-hand. You can also pick up germs from touching a menu, a doorknob, the buttons on an ATM, and a thousand other places.

The solution? Either lock yourself in a sterile environment and never meet other people, or, as suggested by the latest medical studies, simply wash your hands before you eat or touch your face.

Combined, our more than sixty years in sales and etiquette have taught us that the more you put into something, the more you will get back. And no detail, including the handshake, is too small to focus on. We are convinced that anyone who doesn't know what he or she is handing a client when reaching out to shake hands is not at peak performance.

You may already be a world-class hand shaker. If you are, great! This book will reinforce things you already know, and help you increase your message-sending and interpretive skills. If you shake hands every day and think little of these exchanges, then this book can really have an impact on your social and business life.

Most importantly, we believe this book will increase your awareness of your own handshake and how it affects the image you project to others. That knowledge will lead you to discoveries about other people. It can lead you to tap into your intellectual resources, which leads to making the most of your introductions and to successful interactions. It will prevent you from walking away from a greeting empty-handed.

In summary, we believe that eyes may be the doorway to the soul, but the hands are the doorway to a successful encounter.

—Robert E. Brown and Dorothea Johnson

CHAPTER ONE

THE HANDSHAKE:

HUMAN RITUAL AND POWERFUL COMMUNICATION TOOL

The two shook hands, sizing each other up, looking deeply into each other, and in a moment each was

satisfied, and Tom said, "Well, I see you have been busy."

—JOHN STEINBECK, *The Grapes of Wrath*

THE POWER IS IN YOUR HANDS

Over the millennia, Westerners have developed handshaking as a simple ritual of greeting and parting: the extension of right arms, the clasp of hands, the shake and release. To the casual observer, handshakes appear like quotation marks, punctuating conversations. They open the door for discussion with a show of good will, and close it with an agreement or dismissal. But closer scrutiny reveals much more than that. Because of the widespread acceptance of the ritual, handshakes are almost impossible to avoid. They are as integral to making a first impression as your clothes, your smile, your eye contact , or your opening remarks. Even though required in our daily meetings, the subtle power of handshaking quite often goes unnoticed.

This power is twofold. First, the handshake is the only socially acceptable situation in which you can touch a stranger of the same or opposite sex without raising suspicion. Fear of sexual harassment has made us increasingly wary of touching one another. There are now "safe zones," like the hand and arm, which allow innocuous interaction. But the handshake provides a vehicle by which our human need to come in contact with one another can be fulfilled.

Second, handshakes reveal inner traits, personality, and motivations. The hands can't conceal messages as the spoken word can. Your hands are messengers of your subconscious mind, and whether you like it or not, your handshake will often betray your emotional state.

Handshakes reveal a vast array of feelings: sincerity or insincerity, dominance, submissiveness, inferiority, apathy, and deceit.

Whether you're giving or receiving a handshake, there is usually something to be learned from it. Have you ever received a painful, bone-crushing handshake? What was your reaction to it?

Have you ever extended a sweaty palm for someone to shake? Were you embarrassed about it? How did you think that person interpreted your offering? Though there could be other explanations, the bone crusher was probably trying to dominate you, and the person receiving your moist handshake probably sensed your nervousness.

Just as powerful as a handshake itself is its omission. Have you ever refused to shake someone's hand? Or have you engineered your way out of a handshake by grabbing your purse, a cup of coffee, or some other object? Why? Has anyone ever refused to shake your hand?

If you refused to shake hands, you probably did so because you wanted to insult or reject a person. This could occur anywhere: in the courtroom, on the tennis court, or on the football field. But most of us, at some time or another, have experienced the bitterness of either refusing or being refused the acknowledgment of a handshake.

When you don't believe someone is telling the truth, you may sense that his body language doesn't match what he's telling you. While he is saying one thing, his eyes or hands are expressing something else. This comparison of verbal and nonverbal communicators is often possible through a handshake.

Why shake someone's hand anyway? Why not just say hello and smile, raise an eyebrow, state your purpose, and get on with it? Why clasp right hands and "pump" a few times?

Elaborate forms of greeting and leave-taking are characteristic of human behavior throughout the world. Though they seem to be almost unconscious acts, salutations have been important since early man established himself as a hunting species. The male left the group at a specific time and returned with the kill. These displays became necessary, both when the group divided and when it came together again. Since the success or failure of the hunt was vital to the communal life of the tribe, these ceremonies of greeting and parting carried great weight.

Though all humans practice greeting rituals of some sort, they vary widely in different cultures. Chinese and Japanese hold their hands to their sides and bow; Indians press their hands together in a praying position and tilt their heads to one side; Maoris in New Zealand rub noses; the French kiss both cheeks.

Our greetings have been adapted to our lifestyles throughout Western history. Greek men, in a society where women were sub-citizens, developed a rather curious custom. Upon meeting another man, they clasped each other's right lower arms and touched their own testicles with their left hands. This was probably a symbol of honesty. In fact, the word *testify* is derived from *testicle*. In pre-biblical times, people swore not on the Bible, but on their manhood, that is, their testicles.

WHY MASTER THE HANDSHAKE?

You have no doubt been shaking hands for many years, and nothing unforeseen has happened. So why should you bother to learn—and practice—a technique for something you already know how to do? Time for the inevitable sports metaphor.

No professional tennis player goes into a match without at least two kinds of serves: one he hopes will be an ace and another he's sure to get in on the second service. Each serve has a few basic elements: the toss, the topspin, the footwork, and the follow-through. A professional will practice and practice this until it is part of his muscle memory. The more he does it, the more those fundamentals emerge as large overriding concepts.

Professional athletes improve their performance by practicing every aspect of their sport in detail. You will improve your dealings with other people by practicing every aspect of communication, especially the initial meeting and first impression, as well as the departure.

For most people, including salespeople, doctors, lawyers, politicians, job hunters, and just about everyone who has or wants a job, the fundamentals to prepare and practice are appearance, eye contact, verbal message, and, just as important, the handshake.

With practice, your right hand becomes your automatic sensor for discovering the type of person with whom you are dealing. Time is of the essence, and critical decisions can and will be made based on information exchanged during that first encounter, that first handshake with your client. While a good handshake might not get you a job or a sale, a bad handshake certainly could lose one for you. Research shows that a deal can, more often than not, be predicted by that opening handshake. After that, everything else is a mere formality.

All of this applies to social as well as business situations. Whether on a first date or at a meeting with an old friend, you will benefit from a practiced, well-thought-out first contact.

HANDSHAKING HISTORY

The ritual of shaking hands arose sometime during the Roman Empire, not out of courtesy and good will, but out of fear. The human past was one of danger, where wild beasts and bandits roamed and men walked around well-armed. You carried a club, or as technology advanced, a sword or a gun. All strangers immediately aroused suspicion.

When you met a stranger, you had a number of choices. Both of you could turn and run back in the direction from which you came. Both of you could stand your ground and fight. Both of you could clutch your weapon more firmly and proceed on your way, giving each

other the widest possible path. Or, you could remain peaceful, and perhaps, become friends.

In order to become friends, you first had to make sure the other man would not attack. You either laid down your weapons or kept your right (dominant) hands away from them, displaying empty palms. (Because left-handedness was considered evil in those days, you exposed right hands.) To be certain neither of you would grab his sword and lunge, you grasped right hands. Thus the handshake was born—not of friendship but of mistrust.

Handshaking for women came much later. Until the last fifty years, typical greetings between a man and woman included the man tipping his hat and kissing or bending over a woman's hand, and the woman curtsying.

Raising your hat to a lady dates back to the age of chivalry. Knights in armor lifted their visors to show they were not afraid of being

7

attacked. Eventually, it became the custom of a knight to stand bareheaded in the presence of a lady. This is the ancestor of the hat tip.

Before women started shaking hands, the curtsy was the appropriate greeting. A slightly bent knee, lowering of the body, the dress held out to the sides, all kept women at an inferior level. After curtsying, the woman might have extended her hand, often gloved, for a man to kiss. Women had always been exempt from shaking hands and hat tipping, probably because of the male's feeling that he had nothing to fear from a mere woman. A man offering his hand to a woman carried the implication that she too could be dangerous.

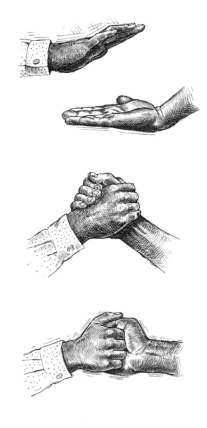

Psychiatrist and scholar Malcolm Stewart-Morris, M.D., believes the acceptance of women shaking hands was an Edwardian development during the 1930s. The participation of women in the business arena has added a new dimension to handshaking. Women now shake hands in business and social situations and face the same opportunities and problems that men do each time they proffer their hands in welcome. One must now be prepared to interpret the same clasp from a man or a woman.

In the past two decades, variations of the handshake have become symbols of brotherhood and unity. The "brother shake" and "high five" are excellent examples of this. The African American power shake (part ritual, part show-off, part ethnic expression, part language) has become a popular, soulful addition to our handshaking vocabulary. It sometimes creates confusion about how to grip someone's hand, either straightforwardly or with the "African American" shake.

High-fiving has become standard among athletes and friends alike in the past two decades. But the athlete's slap, or high-five, didn't originate on an American football field or basket-ball court. References appear in eighteenth and nineteenth century literature describing the slapping of palms to seal a bargain, especially among the French. Strangely enough, an old Irish custom involves spitting in the palm and shaking hands to seal a deal.

CHAPTER TWO

THE TWELVE BASIC HANDSHAKES

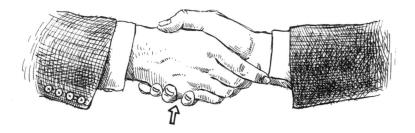

I see you on the street; I smile, walk toward you, put out my hand to shake yours. And behold! —without any command,

stratagem, force, special tricks or tools, without any effort on my part to make you do so, you spontaneously turn toward me,

return my smile, raise your hand toward mine. We shake hands—not by my pulling your hand up and down or your pulling

mine, but by spontaneous and perfect cooperative action. Normally we do not notice the amazing subtlety and amazing

complexity of this coordinated "ritual" act.

—HERBERT FINGARETTE (1967) *describes the act of handshaking*

There are twelve basic handshakes you can expect to receive during your interactions with people. Within and between the different handshakes are many variations, combinations, and alternatives. Everyone is unique. Every meeting of two people is a unique situation. Not every handshake you experience will fit exactly into one of these categories (but most of them probably will). As you progress through this book and learn to observe and understand handshakes, you may want to form your own system of handshake classification.

1. ALL-AMERICAN

This is the handshake delivered by corporate executives and champions of both genders. This person makes eye contact, smiles, offers a firm grip, and two or three

strokes. The handshake delivers a feeling of relaxed self-confidence. This is a warm and genuine greeting acceptable worldwide.

2. LINGERING

This handshake is firm with a warm grasp, with two or more strokes similar to the All-American shown above. The end of the handshake is done almost in slow motion, though, and it lingers. This person is not intimidated by you. This is revealed in the confident hesitation at the end.

While the All-American handshake can be considered perfunctory, the feeling you get from the lingering is of openness. The lingering handshake can be sincere.

In some instances, the lingering may make you feel a little suspicious, as if this person has something up his or her sleeve. Does the person want something from you? Is this why he or she won't let go?

Another possibility is that the individual is intentionally pausing at the end of the handshake to reinforce a message and read your reaction, or the person wants to be there to discover who you are. We'll cover this later in the book.

3. PUSH-OFF

This grip could be firm and warm, but at the end, your hand is flicked away. The extent of the push-off varies, but it implies the need to establish territory. At the harmless end of this spectrum, a person is giving you a slight stiff-arm to keep you out of his intimate zone. The other end of the gradient is a flat-out rejection. This person is not interested in what you have to say. You leave the handshake feeling rebuffed.

This handshake should tell you to respect that person's territory. If it is flat-out rejection, you must ask yourself how much effort you are willing to put into this meeting or if you should find a way to regroup and approach this person from a different angle.

4 . PULL-IN

The opposite of the push-off is the pull-in. This person holds onto your hand and guides you in a direction. It could pull you in, toward the handshake, or direct you somewhere through a door or toward a chair. This is a clever, manipulative handshake and is usually a sign that the person is maneuvering you. He has accepted you and wants to place you somewhere.

Rather than feeling comfortable with people only when they are at a safe distance, the puller is at ease when you are within his own personal space. He is either a bit domineering or he may be from a culture with a small intimate space and, in keeping you close, is merely behaving normally.

The extreme variation of this handshake is *the spider*, which wants to pull you into his web and keep you there.

5 . TWO-HANDED

The right hand grabs yours, but the left hand tells the story. The left hand is manipulating—pushing, pulling, covering, directing—as it takes its place somewhere else on your body. The common left-hand positions are on the wrist, forearm, biceps, shoulder, or neck. The higher the left hand moves up, the greater the manipulation and control. A hand clasped around the neck connotes a perception of intimacy or ownership.

Coming from someone you barely know or have just met, the two-handed shake should arouse your suspicions. Anyone who wants to be in a winning position will use the two-handed or glove shake. Though it is meant to imply sincerity, it is nothing less than manipulation, and the favorite of politicians.

However, the two-handed grip can also be used to strengthen a bond. It is often used by ministers, close friends, and older people, and is especially effective when conveying sympathy. Dr. Effie Chow explains that a four-handed shake forms a figure eight, which allows the maximum amount of energy to flow through the handshake. This should be used only with people you know well.

Louise Howard, co-owner and director of Gold's Gym in San Francisco, described a two-handed handshake she once received. "I shook hands with Charlton Heston at a wedding reception. I've never felt so B.S.'d in all my life," she said. "It was the attempt at the warmest, nicest handshake, and I just felt like there was nobody there." The actor was in a receiving line, meeting a large number of people, shaking everyone's hands the same way. What struck her was that she thought he wouldn't have remembered who she was two

minutes later, and the sincerity was feigned. Had there been no pretensions, Heston would have preserved her respect.

On the other hand, Greg Lamond related how a two-handed shake affected him very positively. Lamond had been working on Hubert Humphrey's presidential campaign in 1968, and shook hands with the candidate in a receiving line. His reaction was very favorable, and he thought the politician's grip was extremely sincere.

Bob Brown relates the story of being invited to attend the San Francisco Bible Breakfast Club in the early 1960s. "The cast of characters was fascinating. Mayor Christopher presided and it was common to meet people like Ken Kesey, who wrote *One Flew Over the Cuckoo's Nest*, or Wally Kibby, a San Francisco printer who believed he was the reincarnation of Ralph Waldo Emerson—I believed it also. Frequently, I would be seated next to Benny Bufano, the sculpting giant. I vividly recall the first time we shook hands. The tip of the first finger on his right hand was missing. It turns out that Bufano severed his trigger finger and sent it to President Wilson to protest World War I."

6. THE TOPPER

This handshake says, "I'm in charge, I'm the Boss." It tends to be the handshake of the conventional boss or manager who manages through control.

The dominant party in this handshake has his or her palm facing down in relation to the other person. Like the winner of an arm-wrestling match, the hand on top is clearly in control. If the person is too controlling, this can limit his or her effectiveness with other people. An equalizing counter for the topper will be explained in a later chapter.

7. FINGER SQUEEZE

Like the push-off, the finger squeeze is used to keep someone at a comfortable distance. There's nothing warm or inviting about it. On the extreme end of the finger squeezer is the bone crusher, an insecure person who equates brute strength with personal power.

Bone crushers are the modern incarnates of Neanderthal Man, who still have the uncontrollable instinct to dominate and overpower people. Their hands are weapons, used to crush any possible threat from the outset.

San Francisco Superior Court Justice Ollie Marie-Victoire tells the story of an Australian judge she met who greeted her so enthusiastically her hand ached long afterward. Two days later she saw a doctor, and to her dismay, found out her fingers were broken!

Penny Patterson, of The Gorilla Foundation in Woodside, California, had quite a different experience with a brute. One day Koko (the world-famous female lowland gorilla) brought Penny's hand very close to her face. Penny had a sliver in it that she had not been able to get out herself. Koko, with her gigantic hands, plucked the splinter from her trainer's hand.

You can judge for yourself who does and does not know his or her own strength. But behind most finger squeezers and bone crushers is an insecure person, who wants desperately to assume authority.

Dorothea Johnson met Secretary of the Navy John Warner (now Senator Warner), in 1972, at Quantico Marine Base, Virginia, after the graduation ceremony of Command and Staff College Officers. "I noticed that he wore a black glove on his right hand and did not shake hands with the officers or anyone present. During a brief conversation, I observed him holding his right hand with his left hand and he appeared to be in pain. I asked if his hand bothered him and he replied, 'Oh, yes, let me show you the results of shaking hands with about a thousand midshipmen at the Naval Academy two days ago.'" The Secretary removed his glove to show Dorothea a badly bruised and swollen hand.

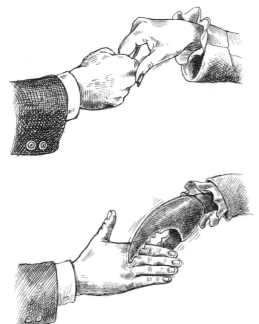

8. PALM PINCH

Unlike the finger squeeze, the palm pinch is not an aggressive engagement. This person offers two, maybe three fingers. It is typically delivered by a woman who has not learned to shake hands or has a fear of interaction. No palm-to-palm contact or energy transfer occurs in this handshake.

Pinchers come in three types. One is very timid and hopes to avoid all physical contact and get the whole thing over as soon as possible. The second is the provincial woman who has been schooled to present a man with only the fingertips of her hand. The third is delivered by a man to a woman when he wants to emphasize that he considers her a woman, even through his handshake. By shaking her fingers only, he is denying her the same fully engaged clasp he gives a man. This clearly says, "You're a woman."

9. TWISTER

In this one, the shaker grabs your hand and twists it under his. This places your hand in the submissive position. This person is saying: "We're coming into this even, but in the end I'm going to be on top and you'll be on the bottom." The twister is the most aggressive type of handshake because it gives you the least chance of bringing the shake to equal terms. Look for the hidden agenda. A counter for the twister will be explained in a later chapter.

10. ROYAL

Like the pincher, the royal handshake is an obvious avoidance of interaction. Some dignitaries suffer through hundreds of handshakes per day and have developed light, almost invisible clasps. This is the handshake you might receive from a queen or duchess, a woman still living in another era. The purposefully aloof clasp asks: "Do you *know* who I *am*?"

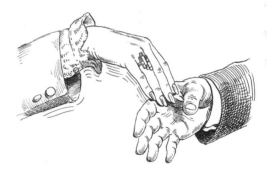

There was at least one royal figure, however, who was a renowned world-class hand shaker. On a trip to New York, Princess Diana spent a few days of relentless greeting and receiving. The night after she arrived, in the receiving line at the Brooklyn Academy of Music, she shook 135 hands. The next morning, outside the Henry Street Settlement, there were 38 hands to shake. At a dinner party for the British Knitwear Company, there were 150; a stop at a homeless shelter the next day required 202; and a visit to the children's AIDS ward at the Harlem Hospital involved another 59 handshakes. In just two days, the Princess shook hands no less than 584 times! Lady Di had an extraordinary ability to earn the respect of people worldwide. Handshaking may have played a big part in it.

Judging from film archives, Princess Diana gave a true "All-American Handshake." However, in her case, the handshake should be renamed the "United Nations Handshake."

If you are a person who shakes a lot of hands, don't rush or treat it as a chore.

11. WATER PUMP

This person pumps your hand like he or she is drawing water from the well. The initial good feeling evaporates after the fourth or fifth pump. Though the average handshake can include from two to seven pumps, there is a point of diminishing returns. In *The Hand Book*, Lee and Charlton assert that Midwesterners, especially people of Germanic origin, enjoy giving

extended, five- or six-stroke handshakes. Easterners, because of busy schedules and the Anglo-Episcopalian inhibition against prolonged touching, give the shortest handshakes, either one stroke (down-up) or, occasionally only half a stroke (down.)

After the original connection is made, don't pump your way out of it.

May the road rise to meet you. May the wind be always at your back. May the sun shine warm upon your face, the rains fall soft upon your fields and, until we meet again, may God hold you in the palm of his hand.

—IRISH BLESSING

12. DEAD FISH

No one likes to receive the dead fish. It is cold, clammy and indifferent. This person doesn't even muster the energy or interest to give you a real handshake. It drains you. The dead fish is an excellent example of the passive personality, with little or no self-esteem. It says, "Not only am I relinquishing responsibility for myself, I'm transferring my apathy to you." According to Luann Lindquist, "This is a temptation to the co-dependent personality who will, in the case of the dead fish, jump at the opportunity to fix it. A healthy response to a dead fish is to get rid of it fast; it only gets worse."

CHAPTER THREE

GREAT HANDSHAKES
AND HOW TO GIVE THEM

Dazed by a confused feeling of pleasure and rage, she gave him her hand for the first time and only then did Mauricio Babilonia

let himself shake hers. Meme managed to repent her impulse in a fraction of a second, but the repentance changed immediately

into a cruel satisfaction on seeing that his hand too was sweaty and cold.

—GABRIEL GARCIA MARQUEZ, *One Hundred Years of Solitude*

PUTTING YOUR BEST HAND FORWARD

Sending your message and simultaneously learning as much as you can about the other person while shaking hands takes some preparation and practice. It involves physical and mental preparation, following the four-step handshake formula, understanding and respecting the other person's personal space, and more if you want to make that all-important first impression a positive one.

FIRST IMPRESSIONS

First impressions are important in all meetings, whether personal or business. The handshake is an important part of making a good first impression and forming one about the person you meet.

PROLOGUE

Judy Smith is a young woman beginning her career as a salesperson. In addition to her basic social, business, and sales skills, she is naturally aware of the power of and the messages in handshakes. As she travels through her personal and business life, she uses this awareness to her advantage.

Judy, along with her friends and family, will appear from time to time throughout this book, illustrating many of the points in the text by telling a story.

~✐~ ~✐~ ~✐~

Judy Smith arrived five minutes early at Argonaut Industries headquarters, a sprawling, glass and cement complex contoured to rolling hills. It's late in the day, and the stale taste of her present job lingers on her lips. Judy's colleagues don't appreciate her extra effort, there's too much hard work for the commission and it has been a long time since she's had a break. A job with Argonaut could be just what she needs.

The glass doors open automatically and she walks into the lobby. A blonde woman appears from behind the reception desk and smiles at Judy. Judy tells her she's there to see Mr. Svenson. The receptionist asks Judy to have a seat.

Judy knows she'll be meeting with Peter Svenson, the regional sales manager for Argonaut. He has seen her résumé and arranged this appointment. Judy rehearses what she's planning to say, what makes her especially qualified, and why she wants the job. Above all, in this first meeting, she wants to make a favorable impression.

She looks around the reception room which is very impressive. The sofas and chairs are covered with luxurious fabrics, which blend with the carpet. Impressive paintings hang on the walls and fresh flowers add to the ambience. Judy reminds herself of the high salary she'll request to allow for negotiating.

Minutes later, while the receptionist leads her down a long corridor, Judy wipes her palm on her skirt to make sure it's dry and silently practices what she's going to say. She repeats Svenson's name a few times to herself to make sure it's on the tip of her tongue. Suddenly, she's in the doorway of his spacious office, and she takes an inconspicuous deep breath. The receptionist nods and smiles, then closes the door behind her.

Svenson rises and walks around his desk to greet her as his eyes quickly sweep over her. His window looks out onto the broad green lawn. With a glance, she takes in the office, his clothes, and his face.

"Mr. Svenson, I'm Judy Smith."

Svenson extends his hand. "Peter Svenson," he says. His voice is strong and confident, but friendly.

She extends her hand, and finds his grasp warm and firm. She makes eye contact and adjusts her grip to equal his strength. He shakes twice and releases.

"Have a seat," Svenson says.

Just from his handshake, Judy feels that he likes her already. He seems sure of himself, which takes the edge off her nervousness.

"Welcome to our new headquarters." Svenson adds.

In the brief moment as they shook hands, Judy and Peter both formed first impressions. They assessed each other's physical appearance, clothes, eye contact, and voice quality. But the handshake gave them the chance to touch, and in that moment, they exchanged valuable information.

Peter's grip was warm and firm. Judy sensed that he was confident and friendly and a mature businessman. It gave her a positive feeling, one of trust, and indicated that he's going to be fair.

If he had shaken hands overzealously, she might have thought him immature. If his hand had been moist, she might have sensed his nervousness. If he had shaken quickly and pulled away, she might have perceived some insincerity or lack of interest.

Business etiquette embraces the handshaking ritual; therefore, it was especially important that Judy's handshake with Peter was firm. This demonstrated that she's capable, assertive, and able to hold her own in the business arena. Had Peter refused to shake her hand, the introduction would not have gotten off to such a pleasant start. He would have kept an aloof, perhaps uncomfortable, distance between them.

Compare Judy's relationship with Peter to her relationship with the receptionist. She didn't shake *her* hand. The two of them exchanged only formal information. The relationship is merely functional. But the handshake between Judy and Peter made a bond, a symbol of acceptance. They both expressed, like the knights of old, fair play and good intentions.

PREPARE YOURSELF MENTALLY

There are a few things you can do to maximize the signals you send and receive during a handshake.

UNDERSTAND YOUR ATTITUDE

First you must have the right attitude. Before meeting someone, *think positive thoughts.* Ground yourself by relaxing. Focus only on the present meeting. First and foremost, get in touch with who you are, and realize that this is the person you will be projecting momentarily.

This orientation process involves acknowledging the *emotional state* you are in at the time you greet someone. What are you feeling? Are you angry about something unrelated to business? Are you nervous or eager to meet this person? Are you feeling like an adult? Or more like a teenager, angry because you haven't gotten your way? Or as innocent as a child? All of these emotions or roles are fine, as long as you are sure they are appropriate for what you want to express at the time. Any sense of doubt or insecurity will come through when you shake hands.

KNOW THE IMPRESSION YOU WANT TO MAKE

Next, remind yourself of the impression you want to make as a result of the meeting. In a business situation, you will be most effective if you project a mature, experienced, professional demeanor.

PREPARE YOUR MESSAGE

Finally, to improve your chances of developing a successful relationship, know the message you want to send before you shake hands. Your message is simply the outcome, great or small, that you want to achieve during the meeting.

Visualize the outcome. Do you want to get rid of this person? Do you want to win him or her over to your point of view? Do you just want to make friendly, comfortable contact? Do you want to express enthusiasm?

Condense the message into one or two words. This simplifies the intention and encapsulates it for sending. The clearer the message is to you, the better your chances of successful transmission. If you can imagine it actually flowing out of your hand through the center of your palm into the other person's palm, then you indeed understand this concept. It may be hard to perceive at first, but with time, you will find that the other person receives your message.

PREPARE YOURSELF PHYSICALLY

You can prepare yourself physically by tapping into your intellectual resources and creating an inner awareness.

DEVELOP YOUR SENSE OF TOUCH

Fine-tune your sense of touch. With practice, your hand can become a sensitive transmitter and receptor. Because of the concentration of various specialized nerves and sensory receptors in the palm and fingers, the hand is able to detect very subtle characteristics and movements of objects.

The hand has more nerve endings per square millimeter than any other part of the body, with the greatest concentration in the fingers. These are highly responsive to texture, rigidity, temperature, weight, and/or size. Pacinian corpuscles are pressure receptors, which respond to vibration and stretch in addition to pressure. Found in the dermas of the skin, they are abundant in hairless zones such as the palms and soles of the feet. These, combined with other factors, make the hand the brain's most important touching and sensing tool. In fact, the palm contains so many essential nerves that, according to Mathias Massem, M.D., forcing an ice pick through the palm would sever the nerves, and render the hand completely useless.

OFFER A DRY HAND

Discreetly, wipe your palm on your jacket to make sure it's dry before extending your hand. Now you're ready to shake.

Clammy hands can be controlled by spraying them with an antiperspirant. It takes at least twenty-four hours to become effective. Spray both hands once a day. Your physician should be consulted for a severe case of clammy hands.

PALM-TO-PALM: THE FORMULA FOR SUCCESS

There are four steps to a great handshake: *Engage, Pause, Observe,* and *Remember.* Follow this simple formula (after proper preparation), and you will make a positive impression you want and gain a better understanding of what the other person is thinking.

ENGAGE

A proper handshake should engage a person's full hand. *Engaged* means far enough in so that the web between your thumb and index finger is touching your partner's web. The hand should be flat enough so your palms are touching. This puts your hand in the position to give and receive messages.

The handshake is an expression of good will, not a wrestling match. Your grip should be firm, but not crushing. A genuine, warm handshake leaves you with a positive feeling. A weak handshake lingers and drains energy from you.

Avoid pinching fingers or cupping the hand. These methods do not allow you to benefit from the exchange that occurs in a fully engaged handshake. They are also obnoxious and evasive.

PAUSE

The pause is very important to mastering the handshake. It is the key ingredient of a successful handshake. By pausing at the natural conclusion of the handshake, you express sincerity and openness.

Focus on the handshake. The objective of the pause is to be the last one to release your hand from the handshake. This will allow you to receive any information your partner may be sending, as his or her hand brushes across your fingers or palm.

As you pause, hold your hand at a slight angle. If the other person were to relax his or her arm, you should have enough strength to hold his or her hand up. Cup your last two fingers under slightly, with enough force to support the edge of the other person's palm. As the hand pulls away, you'll be able to discern a few things about the person.

Being the last one to let go may seem awkward at first. But if you're projecting a positive attitude with the rest of your non-verbal communicators (your voice, eye contact, smiling or restraining a smile, maintaining a comfortable distance between you and the other person), the lingering won't be offensive. At the moment of the pause, you should be as cordial to the person as you have been thus far in your introduction.

You might begin to speak, but concentrate on the handshake at the same time. It is important to remember that concentrating on your sense of touch does not mean watching the hand you are shaking. Avoid lowering your eyes from the other person's face while you are shaking hands. Lowering your eyes dampens the tone and power of your greeting.

If you are a woman shaking hands with a man, you may feel even more reluctant to pause, fearing that your lingering hand could be interpreted as being flirtatious. Don't worry. If you have confidence, you'll project equality through your handshake. There's no reason a woman shouldn't pause just as a man does.

OBSERVE

Pausing allows you to observe the type of handshake you are receiving. Is the person pushing or pulling? Twisting? Damp and lifeless? Shaking vigorously? Is the hand warm and damp? Cold or dry?

Minute muscle movements reveal your partner's emotional state, and in pausing, you will be able to detect them. These muscle movements are set in motion by the unrecognized thoughts of the person with whom you are shaking hands. These are the same movements which are thought to be responsible for projecting the outcome of the Ouija® board, the fall of yarrow sticks, the psychological projections facilitated by the I Ching, or the expression of a handwriting style. Without observing how the other person is shaking hands, you are likely to leave the encounter empty-handed.

Take the process one step further. Alert your subconscious to be aware at the moment you shake hands, and to send the impressions it receives back to you as it sorts and categorizes them. Even if you are too busy at that moment to collect or analyze data, you can subconsciously focus on the handshake at the time of the pause, and the information will come back to you when you need it.

Visualize working on a problem that has brought you to a complete standstill. You have been working on it so hard, you can't tell the beginning from the middle or the end. You walk away from it and beg your brain to come up with the answer. What you are really doing is asking your subconscious mind to come up with the answer and, more often than not, it does. This successful partnership between the conscious and subconscious minds is also highly effective in handshaking.

REMEMBER

Your meeting is over. Can you remember the handshake? Recall and re-create it while you are walking to the car. Focus on particulars. Who shook first? Who let go first? Was the person nervous or relaxed? Did the handshake fit what he or she was saying? Were you unable to react to someone's handshake the way you might have liked to? Compare the opening and closing handshakes. If you remember what you've observed, you can begin acting upon that information.

To remember more easily, create a visual image of the handshake each time you greet someone. If you keep a journal, jot down a brief characteristic of the handshake. Use your imagination, use your own methods, but, by all means, remember.

Small movements and signals transmitted through the handshake can reveal some surprising and powerful insights. We often gain these insights subconsciously, but if you are aware that they exist and learn to sense them, they can tell you even more.

Combining the subtle messages you receive through a handshake along with all the other non-verbal communicators (facial expression, eye motion, tone of voice) will help you form a more complete picture of who the other person is, how he or she feels about you, and what he or she wants.

PERSONAL SPACE AND COMFORT ZONES

Imagine that you have a bubble around you. Inside that bubble is your personal space; the amount of space you need as a buffer to feel comfortable. It swells or shrinks according to where you are and the people you are with.

If you are an American, you probably prefer to keep a significantly large bubble between yourself and strangers. Sometimes, such as when you're in a crowded elevator or on a city bus, the bubble is pressed in on you against your will. When you're around family and friends, your bubble willingly shrinks.

Personal space can be further broken down into different zones that describe how we react, comfort-wise, to various distances from friends and strangers.

The *intimate zone*, a space up to eighteen inches from our bodies, is our ultimate personal space. Only significant people—lovers, family, and close friends—are willingly and comfortably invited in. When others invade this space, we feel less comfortable and often struggle to re-establish it. How do you react when your personal space is invaded in a tight space on a bus, at a ball game, or at the movie theater?

The *personal zone* is the distance you keep between yourself and most of your friends: usually one-and-a-half to four feet. This is typical at cocktail parties or friendly social gatherings.

The *social zone* ranges from four to twelve feet, and is a formal space put between yourself and strangers, such as a person doing repairs in your home, the mail carrier, and similar individuals.

Finally, the *public zone* extends from twelve feet out and is the distance at which you comfortably address a large group of people.

The amount of space you place between yourself and others may largely be a function of the population density of the area in which you were reared. If you were reared in a sparsely populated rural area, you probably have a larger protective zone than someone from the city. You keep your distance. The city dweller, on the other hand, is accustomed to lines, crowds, and limited space, and probably has a smaller social zone.

Watch how far an individual extends the arm to shake your hand. As a general rule, the straighter the arm, the more protective he or she is of personal space. A straight-out arm extension is most typical of

a rural person. According to Allan Pease, a rural person can have zones of four feet or more, while city dwellers have an eighteen-inch bubble. The city dweller steps forward to shake hands, elbow cocked, the arm not fully extended. At eighteen inches, the hands meet on neutral territory, just outside a person's intimate zone. A rural person, however, plants his or her feet firmly and leans forward to greet you, arm straight and extended. Compare young people in a less populated area, waving to each other from distant yards, with inner-city youth crowded together, performing a secret handshake.

Judy got the job with Argonaut, and now, two weeks later, her life has taken a new turn. She drives her Argonaut company car to her first sales call for her new company. She's bought herself a designer suit and good quality leather shoes. Life is good and she's ready to take on the world.

The call takes her to Minotaur Inc.'s headquarters for an appointment with Larry Trout. She has prepared herself for the meeting, and she relaxes, ridding her mind of nervousness and telling herself she is going to sell Trout on Argonaut. In addition to reminding herself of Trout's name and her goals, she prepares for a friendly-yet-businesslike handshake and making a positive first impression.

Trout's secretary escorts her into his office. Trout is a slight man in a blue suit that hangs on his shoulders like a cardboard box. His desk is a mahogany table positioned against the wall, and everything is in perfect order. Trout, it appears, is a very tidy man.

He extends his hand to Judy with his arm straight out, keeping her at a reasonable distance. He grips her hand and releases it immediately, leaving her hand suspended in midair.

This is her first call as an Argonaut employee, and she's eager to get her message through to him, but her mind goes completely blank. She steps closer to Trout, trying to be friendly. He steps back.

"Pull up a chair," he says.

Instead of sitting opposite him, she decides to take the chair next to his. But when she does, he slides his chair back and away from her. While she awkwardly recites her rehearsed lines about Argonaut, his face grows tense. His brow knits into three deep ridges. He's staring at a space on the wall, and his pupils are getting smaller.

Trout speaks. He's sorry, but he's not very interested.

As she's walking back to the car, a thought pops into her head: he's from the country. Now that she thinks about it, she can hear it in his voice. Of course! He told her that with his handshake, the way he purposely kept his distance . . . and the way he reacted when she moved too close.

Had Judy taken the chair opposite Larry Trout, he would have been able to maintain his comfort zone, and her conversation with him would probably have been much easier and perhaps more successful.

As you learn about different types of handshakes and the messages they convey, the theory of personal zones will become clearer. Zones are important in understanding a person who is either pushing you away from or pulling you into his or her sphere of influence.

CHAPTER FOUR

UNDERSTANDING AND INTERPRETING HANDSHAKES

Out where the hand clasp's a little stronger,

Out where the smile dwells a little longer,

That's where the West begins.

—ARTHUR CHAPMAN, *Out Where the West Begins*

THE PAUSE THAT REINFORCES

Judy's long-time friend, Francie, is waiting for her at the café. She's at a table by herself, sipping a latté and smoking a cigarette. Francie is a nurse at Universal Medical Center. Her brown eyes brighten when she sees Judy, who bends down and puts an arm around her, pressing cheek against cheek.

"Sorry I'm late," Judy says.

"The play doesn't start for twenty-five minutes," Francie replies.

Judy continues, "It's been so long and I wanted time to talk. I've been so busy since I started my new job."

"Well, now you're here," Francie says. "How is your new job?"

"Fine. Hectic, but fine." A waiter in a white jacket approaches and Judy orders a cappuccino.

"That's what you wanted to talk about? You just wanted to tell me everything's fine?" Francie says and accidentally blows smoke in her direction.

"Francie, are you ever going to quit smoking?" Judy asks.

"I'm not addicted," she says. "I can quit whenever I want. I enjoy it, that's why I do it."

"A nurse who smokes."

"You didn't come here to talk to me about smoking, either," she says.

"I'm sorry."

Francie puts her cigarette out and exhales the smoke upward, just as the waiter brings Judy's cappuccino.

"There's someone else coming to meet us," Francie says.

"Do I know her?"

"Him. He's really nice," Francie says, raising her eyebrows and smiling mischievously. "One of the residents on my ward."

"Really?"

Almost as she speaks, a man appears and pulls a chair over from another table. He smiles at Francie, says, "Hello," and then extends a hand to Judy.

Francie introduces them, "Judy Smith, I'd like to introduce Will Graham."

Judy stands up and shakes hands with Will. He has a very nice, strong handshake, and holds her hand an extra moment, while looking into her eyes and smiling. She can almost feel the energy moving up her arm.

"It's nice to meet you," Judy says.

"Francie's told me a lot about you," he says.

Judy glances at Francie. "I hope she was kind."

Francie shrugs her shoulders and giggles. There's a brief silence, and to keep it from getting awkward, Judy says, "You have a nice handshake, Will."

"Okay," he says with a little laugh, "if you say so, but I've never really thought about it. What's nice about it?"

"Well, it's firm, and that's rare for a surgeon, a musician, an artist, or anyone who relies on their hands to make a living. They often don't like to shake hands because they fear an injury."

Francie interrupts, "I hate to break up this enlightening discussion, but we should go if we're going to make the opening curtain."

Judy drinks the rest of her coffee and leaves two dollars on the table.

Will walks between the two women and jokes most of the way over. He's a very attractive man, but what Judy likes most is the way he laughs at himself.

Halfway through the play, seated between Judy and Francie, Will places his hand on top of Judy's and gives a little squeeze. A warm, excited feeling passes through her. Again, she can sense the energy, and, as she returns the squeeze, she ponders the power of hands touching hands.

Observant handshaking is, after all, people watching. As you refine your pause technique and your ability to analyze and understand, handshakes will become more precise.

OPEN OR CLOSED?

Company representatives shaking hands should try to determine whether the person they are meeting is *open* or *closed*. An open person is willing to listen to what you have to say. Open handshakes are warm, firm, and enthusiastic, like Peter Svenson's at Argonaut. Depending upon their degree of openness, such individuals may even be prepared to sign a contract with you immediately. "Open" does not mean the person is a pushover, but it does mean that he or she has expressed a genuine interest in what you have to say. This person will be relaxed and have a flexible hand, not too hot, cold, or damp. His or her handshake lingers a bit and doesn't pull away. It feels good.

A closed handshake, in contrast, comes in many forms. It can push you away, be very brief, or pinch you. It can be tense and possibly, but not necessarily, damp. The closed handshake is as perfunctory as possible. This person is not overly willing to listen to what you have to say. Convincing him or her to do business with you may not be easy. You will pull away from this handshake not completely satisfied or trusting.

Develop your own scale, from completely open to entirely closed. Calculate your response. For an open person, proceed immediately. Don't waste time on small talk. Tell the person what you are there for. Try to complete the deal. For the closed person, consider a way to regroup. Be alert that this may be a waste of time or the wrong time. At least, this is going to be a hard sell. This could be a signal that you have to find an alternative way of approaching this person.

WHO'S ON TOP?

On an instinctual level, you can have three reactions to a handshake:

1 . This person is trying to dominate me; I'd better beware.

2 . I can dominate this person; he or she is putty in my hands.

3 . I like this person; we'll get along well together.

The *dominant* party in a handshake has his palm down in relation to yours. Like the winner of an arm wrestling match, the hand on top is clearly in control. The palm doesn't have to be parallel with the floor in order to be dominant, but the hand will be angled so that it is on top of the other. In a study conducted by Allan Pease, nearly 80 percent of Australian upper management officials who were sampled not only initiated the handshake, but exerted dominant control by shaking with their palms down.

The *submissive* hand will be underneath, the one whose palm is face-up to some degree. Much as a dog rolls on its back and exposes its belly or throat to show submissiveness to an aggressor, a human will expose his or her palm, face-up. In contrast to dominating a handshake, offering your palm up can be effective if you want to relinquish control to another person, or at least make him or her feel in control of the relationship.

Equilibrium is achieved on the vertical plane. With both hands straight up and down, there is no dominant or submissive party. There is a feeling of a partnership, which is the goal you should try to achieve.

A CLAM OR AN ICE BOX?

A sweaty palm or damp hand usually reveals a nervous person. Sweat is an involuntary reaction of the sympathetic nervous system. We perspire during times of anxiety or pain. It may also be a sign of a physical condition or disorder, such as low blood pressure or low hemoglobin.

A dry, cold hand could make you back off after shaking it. Perhaps this person is apprehensive or timid. Most people associate cold, dry hands with older people. In medical terms this condition signals poor circulation or nerve injury.

A cool handshake has often been associated with a ladylike or gentlemanly manner. Glass hand coolers were used in the Victorian era to reduce puffiness or redness before greeting someone. Young Southern belles, wanting desperately to make a favorable impression, often stood outside their parlors with hands held above their heads so the blood would drain from their hands, allowing them to present their visitors a pale, feminine hand. Today, hand models use the same technique before going in front of the camera.

WHO OFFERS A HAND FIRST?

In the business arenas of America, gender does not play a role in handshaking. A man or a woman may offer a hand first. When one offers a hand and shakes hands easily and often, he or she creates a favorable impression, which influences others to shake hands. The person who offers a hand first has a distinct advantage. He or she is being direct, taking the initiative, and establishing control. These are cutting-edge pluses in the business arena.

Seniority also plays a role in the business arena. One would wait for a senior, older executive to extend his or her hand. In the social arena, the savvy man lets the woman offer her hand first, especially older women.

TO SHAKE OR NOT TO SHAKE?

Some people have a valid justification for not shaking hands. Surgeons, artisans, musicians, and other professionals who depend on manual dexterity for their livelihoods may be reluctant to shake hands. There are also those whose professions require them to get their hands dirty or wet (bartenders, mechanics, garbage collectors), and who decline to shake hands out of courtesy. A person with arthritis, other ailments, or physical incapacities may not want to shake hands, as doing so could cause pain or embarrassment.

Cultural differences can also explain a person's reluctance to shake hands, and he or she may nod or wave. It is important to recognize and respect these differences. Don't insist on shaking hands, but return the greeting gestures politely.

Judy's life has reached new heights, and time is moving so fast she barely has time to appreciate it. Spring in Northern California has never been so lush. The hills are a deep green and covered with fields of brilliant flowers. Driving through her sales territory is a marvelous experience. Most importantly, she's in love.

She's been seeing Will for more than six months now. This time, rather than distracting her, being in love has helped her focus more on what she's doing. Will has taught her a lot about concentrating on what she's doing while working, and relaxing when she's not. Francie had stopped talking to her when she and Will first started dating, but their relationship has recently thawed.

The job with Argonaut is going exceptionally well. Today, Judy will be making a first-time call on Jerry Blake in the warehouse/factory district south of San Francisco. His commercial domain is greater than any of the other contacts she's made and it is the most lucrative possibility to date.

Before she exits her car, Judy checks her make-up and hair, then wipes her palms against her skirt. She tells herself that Blake is going to be convinced by what she has to say and will like her immediately.

Once at Blake's office, Judy has to wait fifteen or twenty minutes before he sees her. She uses the time to read a magazine article on the gardens of England. When he does come out to meet her, he looks like a tough customer. He is good-looking, has a nice smile, and is very fit. It's not that he's the brute-type, but he has a powerful look and feel about him.

When he extends his arm to shake hands, Judy feels that he's approaching her at an angle. His hand twists hers over and keeps it there for a moment. As his hand withdraws, she realizes she's been placed in a submissive position. She wasn't prepared to react, to bring the meeting onto equal terms.

In a split second, Judy decides to make this visit more general than she had originally planned. She feels that if she were to make a deal with Blake now, he would back her into a corner. So, instead of giving him her whole spiel, she uses this meeting to find out what his needs are, and she offers more questions than answers. She opens rather than closes doors and clings tenaciously to her position.

There's nothing wrong with Blake, Judy thinks, during her conversation. He is very intelligent and obviously professional. There is one thing she senses, though: he doesn't like to lose, and he takes every precaution to see that he doesn't. He seems to have everything covered.

Through it all, she sees that there's a niche for Argonaut to fill here. The trick is to figure out how to bring the relationship to equal terms.

"I'll try very hard to help you with all of the needs you've outlined," Judy says, standing up and double-checking the list she's made.

"Of course, it's not only the price I'm concerned about," Blake says. "We need good service. The quality is important, but I already know it's there. We must have a great deal of flexibility." As he finishes speaking, he extends his hand to shake.

Again, it's the sidearm approach.

"We'll see what we can do, Mr. Blake." Judy's hand is twisted under again.

"Jerry," he says.

"Jerry."

On the drive back to San Francisco Judy wonders how she's going to bring Jerry and herself to an equal stance before closing any deals. And she thinks how romantic a bicycling vacation with Will through the gardens of England would be. Will could certainly use a vacation. And the commission from a deal with Blake—if she can accomplish it—would easily cover the trip.

CHAPTER FIVE

DISORIENTING THE BONE CRUSHER AND OTHER DELICACIES

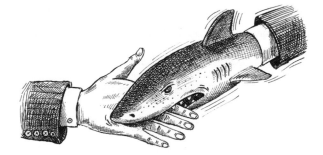

Philip Roth is a good writer, but I wouldn't want to shake hands with him.

—JACQUELINE SUSANN, *after reading* Portnoy's Complaint

HANDLING UNFAVORABLE HANDSHAKES

Judy and Will's wedding reception is an intimate gathering at a bed and breakfast on Alamo Square. The two families have converged from all parts of the country, each taking a wing of the inn. In the process, they've gotten to know each other pretty well without any confrontations.

Though there are only fifty guests, there is still a receiving line with plenty of hands to shake. Judy tries her best not to rush through the process, remaining as open as possible and giving everyone an enthusiastic greeting. Flashbulbs are popping, and shutters are clicking. Judy has been smiling so much she feels like the corners of her mouth are frozen. A man is playing classical guitar, and a jazz band is setting up on the patio. The old Victorian house is full of the smells of food and flowers. It's been beautiful, and she feels that her optimism and buoyancy might just float her away. It has prevailed over the nervousness because everyone seems to be riding the crest of a joyful wave.

Francie is the maid of honor. She's never looked better. As usual, whenever she can get away she's out on the porch smoking a cigarette. She claims she's "in lust" because she met a cute intern at the hospital and brought him along to the wedding.

When Francie comes through the receiving line, he's at her side—a tall, good-looking blonde. She says, "Mrs. Will Graham, I'd like to introduce Dr. Clay Lawton." Then she leans close to Judy and whispers through gritted teeth, "And you're not going to take this one away from me." They both laugh as Judy extends her hand to Clay.

Despite how great he looks, with his surfer's physique and dressed in a suit, Clay shakes with a limp, moist hand—a dead fish—making Judy feel a little uncomfortable.

"It's very nice to meet you," Judy says.

Clay laughs. "Nice to meet you, too."

Judy has to resist a powerful urge to wipe her palm on her wedding dress.

Later, in the bathroom, she and Francie hug and cry in a mixture of happiness and sadness. When they release, Francie asks, "Well?"

"Well what?"

"Clay? What do you think?"

"He's very cute, but I don't know because I just met him."

"But what do you think so far?"

"Well, Francie, remember, we just met for a second, but frankly, I didn't get the greatest feeling from him. I picked up a kind of insecure, needy vibe."

57

After a short silence, while Francie's face wavers from upset to accepting, she says, "Maybe that's why I like him. He needs a lot of attention."

"He's definitely cute," Judy says, trying to lighten the mood. "Should I throw the bouquet your way?"

Francie laughs and opens her purse to find a cigarette.

We have all experienced handshakes that we just didn't like. Maybe they made us feel rejected. Maybe they caused us pain. Maybe they made us want to rush off and wash our hands.

One thing is certain; as you meet more people, there is an increased chance for an unfavorable or unpleasant handshake. The best course of action is to learn how to handle these handshakes and learn as much as you can about the person from them.

ORIENTATION AND DISORIENTATION

While *orientation* involves grounding yourself in your emotions before you shake hands, *disorientation* involves reacting to another person's emotional signals sent during the pause.

By reacting to your observations you can manipulate the situation in your favor. This adds a new element to the formula: *Engage, Pause, Observe, Remember,* and *React.*

If you've been practicing and concentrating on your handshakes, you're probably becoming finely tuned to the art of handshaking as you receive signals every day from people's palms, grips, and motions. In order to make the most of your new skill, however, you have to respond to your intuition.

Perhaps someone is *telling* you with words that he is very interested in what you've said and he'll be happy to get back to you, but you can *feel in his handshake* that he has no intention of doing so. How much effort do you want to expend pursuing that deal? Perhaps someone's handshake tells you he is very defensive and doesn't want his personal zone invaded. Should you ignore his message and invade his space? Perhaps someone is clearly trying to dominate you. How should you respond?

The bottom line is, you can't afford to ignore what you learn from handshakes. It's one more source of information you can use to assess a situation. And reacting to it will give you an advantage.

Disorientation works with Pullers, Pushers, Twisters, and Bone Crushers. Just when the dominant hand shaker thinks he or she has finished with you, let your reaction be *just enough to catch him or her off-guard, and bring the subconscious behavior to the conscious level.* This should be combined with some spoken statement that distracts the focus from the handshake. It requires a great deal of concentration, spontaneity, and creativity. But you can learn to use another person's energy to your advantage.

HAND-TO-HAND TACTICS

Here are some tactics you might use to disorient a dominant hand shaker:

Push-off: If someone pushes your hand away at the end of the interview, it is most likely a negative message. The meeting is over, and you feel rejected. You should consider cutting your losses, and don't put unnecessary energy into calls or letters trying to win that person over. He or she really isn't interested.

That same handshake at the beginning of the interview, however, affords an opportunity to use that push-off energy. As the handshake naturally concludes and you've paused and feel pushed away (by a thrust, a flick, or a push aside), swiftly grasp and hold the hand for a moment as the person begins to withdraw. Don't allow the person to retreat. Say something intriguing: "I have something really great to show you . . . "

This way, you've opened a closing door.

Twister: Though the twister is a rare and extremely overpowering handshake, the antidote is easier than most. When the other person turns your hand to the submissive position, step forward with your left foot, move into the person's personal zone with the right foot, and bring the handshake to equilibrium. Say something to distract and intrigue at the same moment. "I've been thinking a lot about what you said on the phone . . . "

Pull-in: The pull-in handshake, as we suggested earlier, is a spider. A spider pulls you into its web to devour you later. Counter it by allowing yourself to be pulled in by your right hand, then with your left hand, manipulate the hand shaker instead. Give him a two- handed shake and draw both your arms away from his protective zone. Now you're back on equal territory.

Finger squeeze: The finger squeeze is usually an intentional attempt to keep you at a distance. The possibility exists that it was a missed grip. To make sure the greeting gets off to an equal start, ask: "Can we try that again?" and re-shake.

Bone Crusher: The bone crusher is trying to intimidate you. Though there is no physical way to counter this without demeaning yourself, don't ignore it. If you do, you accept that person's insecurities. You might say, "Oh my, your handshake hurts" or "That's quite a grip you have there." In business situations, however, diplomatic decisions have to be made in countering this handshake. There are at least two reactions it can stir in the bone crusher. The first is one of contempt at being chastised for his grip. The second is respect, for standing up to his display of brute strength. Only you can decide how much confronting the bone crusher is worth to you.

~∾~ ~∾~ ~∾~

It's been six months since Judy's first meeting with Larry Blake. She and Will were married, spent their honeymoon in England, and are now looking for a home to buy. Things are going well at Argonaut, better than she ever expected. And even though the initial meeting with Blake was unsatisfactory, Judy hasn't given up on reaching a mutually beneficial arrangement between him and Argonaut.

It's January, and raining, as it has every day for the last three weeks. Judy shakes her umbrella as she enters the building. The receptionist asks her to take a seat in the lobby to wait for Blake. While she sits on the cool leather sofa, she goes over all her notes from the last meeting and sees the one word she wrote about him after the last encounter: twister. She remembers his handshake as if it had happened only yesterday. This time, she tells herself, the handshake is going to be even.

When he finally arrives and extends his hand, she sees it coming: the side arm delivery, then he twists her hand over. But as her hand turns under, she takes a step forward, first with the left foot and then the right. This step places her squarely before Blake just outside his personal zone, and brings both of their hands to an even plane.

The look in Blake's eyes is startled, simply because he's not used to having his hand righted like that. And there was no wrestling involved. The hands came to a natural equilibrium as a result of the step. Just as he recognizes what Judy had done she says, "I'm really looking forward to driving out here again when it's not raining."

Blake smiles. It's a smile that carries respect.

In this second meeting with Blake, Judy disoriented him by stepping into his personal zone and bringing their hands to an even plane. He was no longer the dominant hand shaker he always expects to be. She reacted to her previous observation and brought him from the point of being the dominant person shaking hands to equal ground. This surprised him in a subtle way that earned his respect.

CHAPTER SIX

PRACTICAL AND INTERNATIONAL APPLICATIONS

You can't shake hands with a clenched fist.

—INDIRA GANDHI

TRUE TALES OF HANDSHAKES

Mary Gaynor, an artist and psychic healer in Berkeley, California, often tells this amazing story. While working at the Guggenheim Museum in New York, she was involved with the Venezuelan artist Soto's first one-man show. It was a very complex exhibit, with his pieces appearing throughout the entire museum. As she worked, Soto often watched over her shoulder. He was nervous, because this was a major show for him. But Soto spoke no English, and Mary spoke no Spanish, so they couldn't communicate with each other. When it was all over and he was leaving New York, he came over to thank her for her help.

"I was on the low end of the totem pole, working in the Conservation Department, but I really wanted him to notice me," Mary explained. "In that moment I decided to send him all the love and appreciation I had for his work. I just wanted to get through the language barrier and express my great appreciation.

"As we shook hands, all of a sudden everything went white and golden. Everything disappeared . . . and it was like being in the sun. It was the most astonishing thing because all I saw was light." She was amazed by the connection and, as they released hands, she wondered if Soto also had experienced this. He was standing there, mouth agape, staring at her. In that instant, she realized he had felt the same thing. Then he walked away. "And nothing has happened to me like that since. It was a mystical moment."

Frank Rackley, a retired police officer, was on the receiving end of a powerful message. He remembers shaking hands with a man he'd been trying to convince for four-and-a-half hours to turn himself in and release his hostages. When he finally came out, the man handed Rackley his guns, handles first. As Rackley took the guns, the man reached for his hand to shake it. As they shook, Rackley felt an overwhelming sensation that the man was thanking him for taking the pressure off of him and for putting an end to the crisis. "The man's hand was extremely damp," Rackley said, "and I let go first."

Helen Keller, blind and deaf from birth, was reputed to have been able to recognize people from their handshakes alone for up to two years after a single meeting with them.

Doris Brown, the author's wife, shares an interesting handshaking story:

She worked in the Office of the President of the University of California, one of the largest employers in the state, with approximately two thousand employees. Over a period of years, she had the opportunity, on a monthly basis, to meet all the chancellors of the ten campuses when they gathered at the Office of the President.

Her many interactions with these chancellors involved giving directions to various locations, calling taxis, providing supplies, or just exchanging greetings. One chancellor, however, never noticed her at her desk, not even making eye contact, and she felt somewhat ambiguous about this man.

In the fall of 2003, this particular chancellor was appointed President of the University. During his first week in office, he invited the University of California Office of the President's (UCOP) staff, floor by floor, to meet with him. About two hundred people came together at their designated times to greet the new president. He shook hands with each employee at that time. My wife was most impressed that this man took the time to offer his hand to everybody. That was the first observation and positive sign she noted.

When it was her turn to shake his hand (knowing that she would use the Engage, Pause, Observe, and Remember technique), she congratulated him and wished him well. During their exchange of a couple of sentences, he firmly engaged her handshake and did not let go of her hand during their short conversation. Doris is usually very aware of her surroundings and notices what goes on around her, but she was surprised to find herself noticing just the new president and his presence; the other people in line waiting for their turns became invisible.

Her feelings and observations about this man, whom she had formerly described as distant, aloof, and reserved, changed completely. She now describes him as very warm and friendly, extremely personable, and a great communicator with a good sense of humor.

CHILDREN AND HANDSHAKES

An adult is a role model to a child; therefore, the handshake should express sincerity and politeness. Your message should be that this is a handshake you can use now and when you are an adult.

Michael Pritchard is a counselor, social worker, and comedian, whose work has brought him together with children from all walks of life. Pritchard's PBS television series took him throughout America, talking with teenagers about the problems of growing up. While working with children for more than two decades, he developed a trick he often uses on younger children. Holding their fingers with one hand and rubbing their palms with the thumb of his other hand, he tells a make-believe fortune.

"It's just a very pleasant experience for them," Pritchard explains. Massaging their palms relaxes them and makes a powerful connection. More often than not, when he's finished with one hand, children ask him to do the other. When children want to slap hands or high-five, he requires a full handshake, because he feels it's a more powerful communication. And, he adds, "the children really respond to it."

Pritchard had a story to offer, which he admitted was a bit "Twilight Zone-ish" but one that illustrates the power and possibilities of messages relayed through the hand. Through his counseling, he met a little girl at the Ronald McDonald House. She was a beautiful seven-year-old dying of cancer. She lived much more intensely than other people and seemed capable of living a year in a single day.

Hers was a prolonged and painful illness, and over a four-year period, she underwent bone marrow transplants and chemotherapy. It seemed so cruel, that Pritchard, a person of great faith, began questioning God's mercy. The night he was scheduled to do a TV show in South Bend, Indiana, on suicide and depression, he was informed of the young girl's death. A deep depression followed, and he didn't feel worthy to be talking to kids about the positive aspects of life. Just as the show was about to begin, Pritchard said, he felt a small palm and fingers on his shoulder. There was obviously no one behind him, but he felt the hand press down on his shoulder, then push off and disappear. At that moment, an overwhelming sensation of peace and fulfillment swept over him. It was a restoration of his faith. That night's show turned out to be a great success.

Will is standing on a ladder in front of the kitchen cabinets, handing glasses and dishes down to Judy. They are moving to England. Argonaut has promoted her to director of their new European offices, headquartered in London. Will was able to get a position as a visiting surgeon in a nearby hospital.

Even after seven years, she is continually surprised at the way Will compromises his own needs for her wishes. He does it so easily sometimes she thinks he could leave his career behind to stay home and take care of their children, Matthew, four, and Katie, eighteen months.

"Should we take this or store it?" Will asks, holding a crystal punch bowl they received as a wedding present.

"Store it, I think," she says. He agrees. She wraps it in packing bubble and places it in a box earmarked for storage.

"I got the strangest handshake today, Will," she says.

"What do you mean?" he asks, reaching into the back of the top shelf.

"The handshake said 'get lost.'"

"A handshake said 'get lost?'"

"Yes. He acted really nice and seemed interested and said he'd be getting back to us when he worked out a proposal and the details. But when he shook my hand at the end of the meeting, he just pushed me away, and somehow I knew he didn't mean a thing he was saying."

"Maybe he just wasn't a good hand shaker."

"No. His handshake was fine when we first met."

"Well, maybe he was just in a hurry to go to the restroom or get back to work."

"No. This was a serious meeting. He was telling me to get lost."

"How do you say 'get lost' with a handshake?" Will asks.

She walks over to the ladder, reaches up and takes his hand, then flicks it away at the last moment.

"Hmmm," Will says.

"After he did that, once I was out of his office, I instinctively threw his card in the trash can, despite all the positive things he said during our discussion."

"You don't think there is a chance to salvage the deal?"

"Not a chance."

The sound of Matthew crying in his room upstairs gets their attention.

"I'll go," Judy says, then climbs the stairs to Matthew's room, where the orange nightlight is glowing through the space at the bottom of the door.

Matthew is in his bed and still sobbing. "I don't want to go," he says. "I don't want to go, Mommy, I don't want to."

Judy embraces him and says, "Don't be afraid, Matthew. It's going to be okay."

"I don't want to go," he says. "Why do I have to go?"

She takes Matthew's tiny hand in hers and massages his palm with her thumb. She moves her thumb slowly, in a circular motion. Matthew's arm relaxes first, and soon he stops crying.

"I'll tell you a story about a little boy who had to leave his home and go to a new place. He went to a new home with his Mommy and Daddy and sister, far, far away, across the ocean. They found a new home. There were toys for him to play with and a school for him to go to. He went to school each day and played and learned wonderful things. One day he met a little boy who became his very best friend." She continues to gently press his palm while she makes up the story, and his body completely relaxes. "Sometimes they pretended they were pirates and sometimes they were soldiers and sometimes they were dinosaurs. They colored books together and ate cookies and made forts and ships and houses . . . "

Matthew has fallen asleep. Judy wonders if moving to England is really going to be too much for him—for all of them. Something deep down tells her no, it's going to be exciting and rewarding for the whole family. She tucks Matthew in again and, leaving the door open slightly, because he's afraid of the dark, she goes back downstairs to the kitchen and joins Will to finish their sorting and packing.

HANDSHAKES AROUND THE WORLD

All people are the same,
It is only their habits that are different.

— CONFUCIUS

Judy's many experiences in the corporate arena in America have taught her the value of a strong handshake. Now, she must learn to diplomatically communicate with her handshake in the international arena. After all, the business of the world is business.

Here we describe briefly how culture-based interaction (handshaking) can affect a global business transaction in a variety of countries. However, one must go beyond the handshake and learn in advance a client's cultural preferences and sensitivities, which must be recognized and respected throughout a business relationship. This segment of the book was created to remind the reader that even a small amount of handshaking knowledge will make a difference when meeting and greeting.

Arab Countries: Men may accompany their light and lingering handshake with an embrace and kisses on both cheeks. Follow your host's lead. Arabs stand very close to one another when talking. Women generally are not involved in the business arena, and do not socialize with males who are not family members. Handshaking is normal with Arab women who often travel to Western countries; however, it is not their custom in Arab countries.

Argentina: Men may hug each other (*abrazo*), and women shake hands with both hands and kiss each other on the cheek.

Austria, Greece, Portugal, Spain, and Switzerland: Shake hands with everyone, upon both greeting and departure. The handshake is firm with good eye contact.

Bangladesh, Pakistan, Taiwan, and Sri Lanka: The Western handshake may be used in these countries, although it may not be as firm as one would expect. Avoid giving or receiving anything with your left hand, which is considered taboo. A bow may accompany the handshake in Taiwan.

Belgium, Luxembourg, and the Netherlands: Always shake hands with everyone, upon both greeting and departure. The handshake is light and brief, with eye contact.

Bolivia: Bolivians shake hands with everyone, upon both greeting and departure. The handshake is firm and eye contact is maintained. Bolivians stand very close to one another when talking. Men may greet their relatives and close friends with a hug (*abrazo*). Women may kiss one another on the cheek.

Brazil: Brazilians shake hands with everyone upon both greeting and departure; they maintain eye contact. Greetings are prolonged with a lingering handshake, embraces, and "air" kisses. Brazilians stand very close to one another when talking. Women kiss one another on the cheek.

Chile: Chilean men shake hands. Women often pat each other on the right forearm or shoulder instead of shaking hands, and may hug or kiss one another on the cheek. Chileans stand very close when talking.

China: The Chinese greet with a bow, nod, wave, and with a light, lingering handshake. Any of these gestures may be used upon both greeting and departure. Wait for the Chinese to offer a hand first, and always greet the senior person first. Their eyes may be averted slightly as a sign of respect. Chinese may also greet you with applause, and you should respond with applause.

Colombia: Colombian men shake hands, upon both greeting and departure. Women do not usually shake hands, but they clasp forearms.

Denmark, Finland, Ireland, Norway, and Sweden: Everyone shakes hands, both upon greeting and departure. The handshake is firm but brief and eye contact is made.

Ecuador and Peru: Men shake hands, upon both greeting and departure, and they may embrace. Women who are friends kiss one another on the cheek.

France: The French shake hands with everyone, upon both greeting and departure. The handshake is light and brief. A man may offer his hand to a woman, and he may "kiss" the top of a woman's hand. Friends and family may hug and kiss both cheeks.

Great Britain: A light handshake is standard in business. One shakes hands upon both greeting and departure from a meeting or when visiting a home; however, a handshake is not always correct at social gatherings. Be aware of what others are doing. A man waits for a woman to offer her hand first. The English do not consider themselves Europeans.

Germany: Germans shake hands with everyone, upon both greeting and departure. The handshake will be firm but brief. Never leave one hand in a pocket when shaking someone's hand or when speaking. It is considered very rude.

Italy: Italians shake hands with everyone, upon both greeting and departure. The handshake is firm with good eye contact, and may be accompanied with a grasp of the arm with the other hand. A man waits for a woman to offer her hand first.

Japan: The Japanese greet with a bow and a light handshake. Protocol requires that a bow always be returned with a bow. A slight bow or a nod of the head and eyes cast down is an acceptable greeting from Westerners. Failing to acknowledge a bow with a nod of the head or a slight bow is akin to refusing a handshake. The bow in Japan is used to express respect, appreciation, apology, and congratulations. The Western-educated Japanese will shake hands and make eye contact, as it is more common in the business arena.

Malaysia: Handshaking is not common; however, you may find handshaking in a business meeting with Westerners. Wait for a senior person to initiate the handshake, which will be light.

Maldives, Macau, Indonesia: The Western handshake may be used in these countries, although it may not be as firm as one would expect. Avoid giving or receiving anything with your left hand, which is considered taboo.

Morocco: Men shake hands when greeting. The handshake is light and one might touch the heart after the handshake to express pleasure at seeing the other person and/or to show personal warmth. Close friends and relatives greet by brushing or kissing both cheeks.

Nigeria: There are a large number of ethnic groups so customs vary; however, wait for a senior person to initiate a handshake.

Paraguay: Men and women shake hands, upon both greeting and departure, and kiss twice when meeting with family and friends.

Russia: Russians greet one another with a firm handshake, and relatives and close friends are greeted with an embrace and kisses on both cheeks. Never shake hands over a threshold as it is considered bad luck; always step into the room to shake hands.

Singapore: Singapore has three major ethnic groups: Chinese, Malay, and Indian, and each group has its own cultural and religious traditions. A handshake is the most common form of greeting with younger or Western-educated Singaporeans.

- **Chinese:** Men shake hands with other men, and may shake hands with a Westernized woman. The handshake tends to be softer and longer. It is also acceptable for a woman to nod when greeting a man.

- **Malay:** Contact between men and women is avoided in the Muslim culture, and men do not shake hands with women. "Salaam" is the Malay greeting, which is accompanied with a deep bow with the palm of the right hand on the forehead.

- **Indians:** Contact between men and women is avoided in the Hindu culture, and men do not shake hands with women. The traditional Indian greeting is called the "namaste"—the palms of both hands together at the chest, with a slight bow of the head.

South Africa: South Africans are very talkative when meeting each other. Conversation is accompanied by handshaking and backslapping.

South Korea: South Korean men greet each other with a slight bow and a handshake. To show respect, support your right forearm with your left hand. Wait for the senior person to offer his hand first. Maintain eye contact with persons of the same level or authority. Women usually nod and rarely shake hands, and they don't shake hands with men.

Thailand: The traditional greeting is the "wai" which is the palms of both hands together with the fingers held upward in front of one's face. However, in business meetings expect that the Western handshake will be used. Wait for the senior person to initiate a handshake.

Turkey: Shake hands when greeting or being introduced to a Turkish man. Wait for a Turkish woman to extend her hand. Shake hands again upon departure. Close friends of either gender may be greeted with a two-handed handshake and/or a kiss on both cheeks. Always rise when an elder enters a room and shake hands with elders first as a sign of respect. The handshake will be firm, and devout Muslims may avoid eye contact as a display of humble behavior. Do not stand with your hands on your hips or in your pockets when greeting or when speaking to others. Turkey is part of Europe, not the Middle East, to Turkish business people and government officials. Never call a Turk an Arab. They do not speak Arabic, nor think of themselves as Arabs. Turks are Turks and technically considered European.

Uruguay: A firm handshake is common upon both greeting and departure. Friends may kiss once on the right cheek.

United States: Businessmen and businesswomen give a firm handshake, a smile, and they make eye contact. In the business arena, gender doesn't play a role, and a man or woman can initiate a handshake; however, at social gatherings, it is prudent for a man to wait for a woman, especially an older woman, to offer her hand.

Venezuela: Men shake hands, upon both greeting and departure. They also greet each other with a hug. Women greet each other with an embrace and a kiss on the cheek.

Protocol: Do your homework before going to another country!

CHAPTER SEVEN

BEYOND THE HANDSHAKE:

ENERGY, HYPNOSIS, AND SUBCONSCIOUS COMMUNICATION

And my voice goes everywhere with you

And changes into the voice of your parents,

your teachers, your playmates,

And the voice of the wind and of the rain.

—MILTON H. ERICKSON, M.D.

We've learned how handshaking is vital to communications in the business arena, but how might an understanding of the human hand and its ability to "talk" translate into other parts of life?

THE ENERGY ARGUMENT

Acupuncturist Effie Poy Yew Chow, Ph.D., R.N., L.Ac., looks at handshaking in terms of energy. She has combined her knowledge of traditional Chinese and Western medicine to develop a unique technique of healing and learning through touch. According to ancient Chinese medicine, there are energy bodies and pathways in the body. These are essential to all functions and are governed by an intricate system of laws.

The center of the palm is what acupuncturists call the Pericardium 8, or in Chinese, the *lao gong*. It is considered a major energy point. Stimulating energy points is one of the oldest methods of Chinese healing. And this is precisely why handshakes can be so important. A handshake is what Dr. Chow calls "an expansive phenomenon." This is because there is a flow of energy between the palms during a handshake. According to Dr. Chow, a firm handshake *tones up* or invigorates energy, while a weak handshake sedates or dissipates energy. Contact between one another's Pericardium 8 could be likened to plugging a cord into a socket. If the hands are in a neutral rather than dominant or submissive position, there is a partnership, equilibrium, a flow.

Though most people aren't aware of it, handshakes are valuable communication tools precisely because of the energy and touch involved. Dr. Chow contends that breaking down your fears of touch and becoming aware of touch will bring you in closer contact with your feelings. The energy released during a handshake is directly related to what you are feeling at the time. Your hands won't lie, and in becoming more aware of your handshake, you'll become more truthful to those feelings.

Western practitioners also consider the hand a valuable communicator and look at it in terms of electromagnetic fields and nerve systems. Dr. John B. Watson, an eminent Harvard psychologist, believed that a great deal of human behavior was electrically induced.  During the 1920s, in one of his many experiments, he hooked electrodes to his subjects' hands, then asked them to imagine they were hitting a nail with a hammer. When they did, the electrode monitor spiked. According to Watson, this demonstrated that the hand reacts energetically to the thought process.

It has long been suspected that the hands disclose the truth. Only an expert fabricator can manipulate his hand movements or other body language to match what he or she is saying. This is precisely the concept behind the lie detector, or polygraph, which monitors heart and breath rate as well as perspiration levels while someone is interrogated. Polygraphs attempt to calculate the *psycho galvanic skin reflex* or flow of current between two different parts of the body, including the hands. They also measure perspiration in the palm, because under stress a person sweats more than usual. During interrogation, for example, the presence of excessive perspiration or electrical impulses is thought to mean there is more to the story than the witness is disclosing.

A few nights later, at a farewell party in Francie's apartment, Judy and Francie are alone in her kitchen.

"Judy, you are the luckiest person I've ever seen," Francie tells her. "First, you have the most understanding, handsome husband, who was, incidentally, interested in me first. Second, you have the cutest children ever procreated. And third, you have a job you like that challenges you. Do you know how many people would die to live in Europe?"

"England," Judy replies. "And they wouldn't be so thrilled if they had any idea of all the work involved."

"But it's so romantic!" Francie almost shrieks. "You are so lucky I can't stand it!" She reaches for her purse and finds her cigarettes. She shakes one out of the pack and gives Judy a guilty look. At least they're lights, Judy thinks.

"I wish I could quit," Francie says.

"I didn't say anything." This is the first time Judy has ever heard Francie talk about quitting.

"I'm desperate."

"You really want to quit?"

She nods and drops the extinguished match in the sink. Judy can't tell if she really means it.

"There's a doctor I've read about who uses hypnosis to help people with smoking problems," Judy tells her.

"What does he do, use a watch?" Francie asks sarcastically. "Sleepy, Francie, you're getting very sleepy. You're going to tell me everything, everything, and when I snap my fingers . . . "

"You should know about this, Francie, you're a nurse. Doctors often use hypnosis."

"I was only kidding. How does he hypnotize his patients?"

"With a handshake."

Francie stares for a second, then shakes her head and smiles. "God, I'm going to miss you, Judy, even though we haven't seen each other that much over the last few years. Just knowing you're nearby is always somehow soothing."

"I'll miss you too."

"Can I have that doctor's number?" Francie asks.

When Francie arrived for her appointment, Dr. Glass met her in the waiting room and shook her hand. He was a handsome man, with a dark beard. Just what she thought a psychiatrist would look like. When she was ready to pull her hand away from the shake, she felt a series of strange finger movements on her hand and she pulled it away. She thought about the rumor that psychiatrists go into the field of psychiatry because they have problems themselves. Maybe he was like that. She was a little nervous about going into his office, but remembered that he was highly recommended by her friend, Judy.

Dr. Glass led her into his office and they talked about smoking. Half an hour passed, and she shuddered to think what it would cost. He still hadn't done anything to help her quit smoking. Finally, he asked her some questions about hypnosis and explained his methods. Francie was really excited at the promise of being cured of her habit. Then he stood up and said he wanted her to come back next week and walked her to the waiting room. He extended his hand to shake, and as they shook hands she knew she liked him a lot.

When she was about to pull away from the handshake, she felt the same strange sensation as before, but this time it prevented her from withdrawing. He was brushing her hand ever so slightly with his fingers, each time in a different place. She didn't know what to think. Just when she focused on his rhythm, she heard him say something.

"I'm sorry. What did you say?" Francie asked him.

Dr. Glass was staring away from her. She got the uneasy feeling that he was looking right through her. Then she felt his fingers moving again. She was riveted. Dr. Glass then looked down at her hand. Francie looked down, too. Her hand was motionless in the air in the handshake position. He nudged it downward very lightly, and the right arm went down by itself. At the same time, he gave her left hand an upward push.

When he was sure Francie was in a satisfactory trance, Dr. Glass took her back into his office and sat her in a chair. She was giggling about something, and he asked her to place her hands on her lap. Francie thought that was very funny. He said she could pretend her hands would answer for her subconscious mind. She could raise her index finger on her right hand to mean "yes" and the left index finger to mean "no." She could raise her right thumb to mean "I don't know" and her left thumb to mean, "I don't want to answer now."

"Let's try a few questions now. You don't have to answer any questions if you don't want to," Dr. Glass said, speaking slowly and clearly. "Do you want to quit smoking, Francie?"

"Yes," she said, and raised the index finger of her right hand.

"We had a telephone conversation the other day," he said. "Do you remember telling me that you want to quit because every day you wake up feeling lousy from the cigarettes you smoked the day before, that you tell yourself you're going to quit but then you smoke; and you hate yourself for being too weak to resist?"

"Yes," Francie said, and again raised her right index finger.

"Do you want to quit because it stains your fingers?"

"Yes," Francie said. This time her left index finger rose.

"Do you want to quit because all of your clothes smell like smoke?"

"Yes," she said, and tapped her right finger.

"And do you want to quit because it's unhealthy?"

Again Francie responded affirmatively with her voice and finger.

"Now for the purpose of quitting smoking only, we're going to distance ourselves in time. Let's say you've quit, and all the physical withdrawal symptoms have passed. You no longer feel like you need a cigarette. This time distortion is only for the purpose of quitting smoking. Do you understand?" Francie signaled affirmatively.

"You have made the decision to quit, and you have quit. The longer you stay away from smoking, the better you feel. Every hour, every day, every week, and every year you stay away, the better you will feel. Time will set you free from your habit."

Francie sat in her chair. She was very relaxed. "How do you feel?" he asked her.

"Rested," she said. "I feel good."

"In a few minutes, you'll wake up. You can remember, or you can forget, or you can feel indifferent to everything that happened here. As I count to three, you'll feel more and more awake. One . . . two . . . three. . . ."

Francie was on the edge of her chair, feeling groggy. "Have I been asleep?" she asked.

HANDS AND COMMUNICATION

Psychologist and professor Vernon Dolphin, Ph.D., in his quest to stretch the conventional boundaries of psychology, once conducted an experiment that involved communication through the hands. He induced a female student into a trance in front of a class of forty students. Then Dolphin arbitrarily selected a person to come up and join her. This young man placed his hand on hers, so their hands were making contact. The instructions to the young woman were, "You will remember much about this person afterward." The young man went back to his seat on tiptoes.

When the young woman woke up, everyone wanted to know what she had learned about this other person. They were particularly eager to see if she even knew who he was.

Dolphin asked her what she remembered. "Who was that person?" he asked.

"I don't know," she said.

"I believe you do," he said. "Wave your hand and pick out the person. And tell me what you know about this person."

The young woman's eyes rolled back, as though she were in a trance, and she pointed to the young man who had placed his hand on hers. Then she said, "I see a little boy far out on a branch on a tree, and the boy is falling."

The class's gaze fell on the young man.

He explained that when he was a boy in Texas, he had an argument with his parents and climbed up into his tree house to get away from them. While he was up there, he was cleaning the tree house and went out on the branches to clean the leaves from a limb. In doing so, he fell and broke his back.

"There were two possibilities to explain the communication," Dolphin explained. "Either through hand contact alone, or mind-to-mind, facilitated through the hands."

TEST YOURSELF TO SEE IF YOU HAVE A GRIP ON YOUR FUTURE

The keys to successful handshaking are the following:

1. Have the right attitude; be enthusiastic. Negative or distracting worries or thoughts will be communicated through your body language when you meet someone, familiar or unfamiliar.

2. Prepare yourself mentally. Have your objectives in mind before you shake a person's hand. *Have a clear intention.* What do you expect to gain from your meeting?

3. Prepare yourself physically. Focus on your sense of touch. Your hand can be an extremely sensitive receptor and transmitter of information. Developing awareness will provide you innate knowledge about the people you are meeting.

4 . Use the *Engage, Pause, Observe,* and *Remember* formula to follow through with effective handshaking.

   a . Engage a person's hand firmly, web-to-web with palms touching.

   b . Pause at the natural conclusion of the handshake, and you can sense any messages the person might have to offer you. Look the person directly in the eyes.

   c . Observe some basic qualities while you're pausing. Is the person pushing, pulling, twisting, pinching, or pumping too much? Is the hand warm or dry?

   d . Remember what you have observed, either by creating a visual image of the handshake, or writing it down in a journal later.

5 . Be aware of personal space issues. Don't crowd someone who needs a lot of personal space. Pay attention and react to his or her cues.

The keys to interpreting handshakes are as follows:

1 . Pause and observe.

2 . Whose hand is on top? Be aware and ready to counter dominance games within a handshake. If someone reaches for your hand with a downward-facing palm, understand their message, "I'm in charge," and be ready to counter the move to

establish equilibrium. Also, be prepared to establish equilibrium with someone who gives a palm up, submissive handshake.

3 . Clam or icebox? Notice the temperature and dampness of the hand to judge the person's attitude and nervousness

4 . Who shook first? Analyze the situation to determine if it's appropriate to make the first move to end the handshake.

5 . To shake or not to shake? Analyze the situation to see if it's appropriate to shake at all.

QUESTIONS

Tap into your critical thinking skills to answer these questions. Write down your answers if it helps you focus on recalling your thoughts.

1 . What type of handshakes do you like to receive? Are they the same kind you give to other people?

2 . Think of a handshake you remember well. Was it a handshake or a refusal to shake hands? What impressed you the most about the handshake and why?

3. What does a clammy hand feel like to you? How do you feel if you shake someone's hand when your own palm is clammy?

4. Who taught you to shake hands? Can you remember the lesson?

EXERCISES

1. Keep a journal. When you keep a journal, try making some quick entries about the customers or clients you call on, and what their handshakes told you at the beginnings and ends of each meeting. Are they open or closed? Dominant or submissive? Firm or loose? Do they push or pull? How far out do they extend their hand when they offer their hand for a shake? How did you feel about the handshake?

2. Practice the engage, pause, observe, and remember formula. Try it with a friend. Role-play to find out what your own handshake is like. Have one person act friendly and open and the other hostile and eager to get rid of you.

3. Break old habits.

It has been said that it takes three weeks to develop a new habit. For many people, breaking their habitual unconscious behavior will take that long. If you have been shaking hands as unconsciously as you tie your shoes for any number of years, you'll have to assault the habit full force. Change is only a decision away.

A well-known exercise requires you to leave your watch at home for a day. Throughout the day, notice how many times you check your wrist. If you are like most people, you will find yourself looking at your wrist a number of times after you have realized your watch is at home.

For the next three weeks, concentrate on handshakes. When you meet someone, instead of concentrating on the face, physical appearance, and voice quality, focus on the handshake. Give every handshake a mental sound or picture with which you can easily identify it. In three weeks, you should begin to see how a person's handshake really matches his or her personality or how it doesn't match at all. You will find that handshakes actually do communicate messages to you.

EPILOGUE

"Flight 137 to New York and London will be boarding at Gate Seven in ten minutes," a voice announces.

Judy can't believe she will be leaving and that she accomplished everything in such a short time. This is better than anything she ever thought would happen to her.

Will is standing by the window holding Katie, hoping the kids will make it through the trip without getting sick or crying. But they've played a lot, so maybe they'll sleep the entire flight.

The high-pitched whine of jet engines reaches their ears. Matthew loves machines and stares at the planes with his usual curiosity. Judy thinks about herself as a child, while looking around for Francie, half expecting her to come running down the corridor for a final farewell, even though everyone has been saying good-bye for the last three weeks.

Will has everyone's tickets and smiles as he comes over. "'Ere we go, Judy, to a brand new country," he says in his best—but not very good—British accent. Katie is sucking her thumb. Judy grabs her carry-on bags and walks over to the line.

A flight attendant greets passengers as they board. Judy decides to give Matthew a lesson.

"Matthew, do you know what thumbs are for?"

Matthew sticks his thumb in his mouth.

"No, they're not for sucking," she says, pulling his thumb from his mouth. "They're for handshaking. If we didn't have thumbs to stop them, our hands would slide all the way up the other person's arm when we shake hands!" She shows him what she means. Matthew giggles.

"When you meet someone, you shake his or her hand like this." She takes his tiny hand in hers. "And you look into their eyes and say, "It's nice to meet you."

Just then, a woman comes out of nowhere and throws her arms around Will. A moment later, Francie releases herself from Will's embrace and puts her arms around Judy.

"I had to say good-bye again," she says.

Francie gives Judy one last hug, and says, "Two days, Judy. Two days!"

"What do you mean, two days?"

"I haven't had a cigarette for two days." She bends down and gives Matthew a hug and pats Katie's head.

"We have to board the plane," Will says.

"I just wanted to say good-bye," Francie says.

When it's Matthew's turn to greet the flight attendant, he bends down and takes his hand.

"I'm Mark Buteo, your flight attendant," he says and smiles.

Matthew shakes his hand, and his words come out in shy peeps. "It's nice to meet you," he says.

Judy looks out of the plane's door one last time before going to her seat. Francie is nowhere in sight.

Then, Judy and her family settle into their seats on a jet bound for England.

BIBLIOGRAPHY

Elsea, Janet G. *The Four-Minute Sell*. New York: Simon and Schuster, 1984.

Erickson, Milton, M.D. and Ernest L. Rossi, Ph.D. *Experiencing Hypnosis*. New York: Irvington, 1981.

Firth, Raymond William. *Verbal Body Rituals of Greeting and Parting*, in J. S. La Fontaine, ed. *Interpretation of Ritual: Essays in Honor of I.A. Richards*. London: Tavistock Publications, 1970.

Fuller, R.M. "Know What You're Handing Them," *American Salesman*. December 1984.

Key, Mary Ritchie. *Nonverbal Communication: A Research Guide and Bibliography*. New Jersey: Scarecrow Press, 1977.

Lee, Linda and James Charlton. *The Hand Book: Interpreting Handshakes, Gestures, Power Signals and Sexual Signs*. Englewood Cliffs: Prentice Hall, 1980.

Morris, Desmond. *Manwatching: A Field Guide to Human Behavior*. New York: Harry N. Abrams, 1977.

Napier, John. *Hands*. London: Pantheon, 1980.

Pease, Allan. *Signals: How to Use Body Language for Power, Success and Love*. New York: Bantam, 1981.

Polhemus, Ted. *The Body Reader: Social Aspects of the Human Body*. London: Pantheon, 1978.

Random House Encyclopedia. James Mitchell, Editor in Chief. New York: Random House, 1983.

Tabori, Paul. *The Book of the Hand: A Compendium of Fact and Legend Since the Dawn of History*. Philadelphia: Chilton, 1962.

Tuleja, Tad. *Curious Customs: The Stories Behind 296 American Rituals.* New York: Harmony Books, 1987.

Wolff, Charlotte. *The Human Hand.* New York: Alfred Knopf, 1943.

ADDITIONAL RESOURCES

Intercultural Press (publisher of international books)

374 US Route 1

Yarmouth ME 04096

Telephone: (866) 372-2665 (U.S. only); (207) 846-5168

www.interculturalpress.com

Dos and Taboos Around the World (series of books by Roger E. Axtell)

John Wiley & Sons

111 River Street

Hoboken NJ 07030-5774 Telephone (201) 748-6000

www.wiley.com

Put Your Best Foot Forward (series of books by Mary Murray Bosrock)

International Education Systems

26 East Exchange Street

St. Paul MN 55101

Telephone: (651) 227-2052

www.marybosrock.com